"Deciding when to mourn or r
a solo journey of introspection
as shame, guilt, and forgiveness. Drumsta's well-paced guide takes
readers inward and into their pasts and turns them into writers and
creators of their own futures."

—BRIANNE KIRKPATRICK, MS, LCGC,
Founder of Watershed DNA

"This is a powerful and important book. Drumsta's vast experience
helping others navigate family tragedies has allowed her to craft an
accessible and honest guide to dealing with these upheavals. Written
with poise, humility, and a deep understanding that everyone's situation is unique, this book will help people give structure and voice to
their grief, thereby helping them heal."

—SEAN HANNON WILLIAMS,
F. Scott Baldwin Research Professor in Law,
University of Texas School of Law

"Being hurt by our loved ones is further complicated by the pressure
society puts on us to blindly forgive them. With her years of experience,
Rebekah Drumsta has laid out a road map for planning and carrying
out a healthy and practical path of healing and forgiveness."

—SAMUEL BURKE,
CNN Anchor & Host of the *Suddenly Family* Podcast

"*When Family Hurts* is a helpful guide for anyone who is hurting from
family relationship issues. This book will help readers explore their feelings, thoughts, and emotions on important and relevant topics, such as
distrust, longing, abandonment, guilt, self-doubt, and anger. The book

encourages the reader to dig deep into their own feelings to address the hurt they have experienced, so that healing is possible. Drumsta's 30-day approach can help guide readers on a path of healing from hurts caused by family relationships."

—DR. MAGDALENA BATTLES,
Author of *6 Hidden Behaviors That Destroy Families:
Strategies for Healthier and More Loving Relationships*

"This short, accessible, and engaging workbook will be very helpful to those experiencing problems in their familial relationships. The modules help establish issues that may be negatively affecting psychosocial well-being, while giving helpful suggestions and tips for underlying solutions. The modules spur needed mental work and appropriate action, keeping the reader engaged and motivated to change for the better. It is highly recommended."

—DR. ROB WHITLEY,
Associate Professor of Psychiatry,
McGill University

"Broken or damaged family relationships can hurt deeper than others because these are the very people who are supposed to love us unconditionally, when others can't or won't. If you've been hurt, abused, or otherwise damaged by your family, then working through the helpful steps outlined in this book may well provide the emotional healing and wholeness that may have been preventing you from living your life to its fullest and truly enjoying interpersonal relationships."

—DR. CLINT HEACOCK,
Host of the *MindShift* Podcast

"Rebekah Drumsta's book, *When Family Hurts,* is a much-needed primer for those embarking on the painful—yet essential—journey of healing from family-related trauma. Her daily meditations and helpful exercises serve as a welcome salve for readers in all stages of recovery."

—ERIC SKWARCZYNSKI,
Host of the *Preacher Boys* Podcast

when family
HURTS
30 Days to Finding Healing and Clarity

REBEKAH DRUMSTA

CLAY BRIDGES
PRESS

When Family Hurts

30 Days to Finding Healing and Clarity

Copyright © 2021 by Rebekah Drumsta

Published by Clay Bridges in Houston, TX
www.claybridgespress.com

ISBN 978-1-953300-89-8 (paperback)
ISBN 978-1-953300-88-1 (ebook)

Special Sales: Most Clay Bridges titles are available in special quantity discounts. Custom imprinting or excerpting can also be done to fit special needs. For standard bulk orders, go to www.claybridgesbulk.com. For specialty press or large orders, contact Clay Bridges at info@claybridgespress.com.

Table of Contents

To the person with a hurting heart.
You are not alone.

Preface

Relationships can be complicated. They can hold us back or enable us to do courageous things. They can harm or heal, weaken or strengthen, build us up or tear us down. And unless you've been stranded on an island and are the only human occupant, you are likely in many different kinds of relationships, specifically within your family.

Many conflicts can strain or break a family relationship:

- Divorce
- Health Issues
- Lifestyle Choices
- Sexual or Physical Abuse
- Faith or Belief Shifts
- Discovery of a Lie or Secret
- Miscarriage or Death of a Child
- Financial Disagreements
- Siding with Another Family Member
- Disrespecting Boundaries
- Parenting Methods
- Cultural Differences
- And more!

When Family Hurts: 30 Days to Finding Healing and Clarity was written out of personal observation, experience, and heartbreak. It was designed to guide you on a self-coaching intensive journey that propels you toward emotional healing by clarifying your needs and establishing relationship goals.

Write on these pages. Underline, circle words, highlight lines, and scribble in the margins and empty spaces along the way. This will be a 30-day documentation of your journey to wholeness. The "Daily Check-In" section is intended for you to track the progression of your emotions and thoughts over the coming days.

Whether you're eager to get started or paralyzed with nerves, know that you can do this! As A. A. Milne said, "You are braver than you believe, stronger than you seem, and smarter than you think."

Rebekah Drumsta

Daily Check-In

What emotions are you feeling? What thoughts keep racing through your mind? Have you made any choices or had a breakthrough? Keep track of your progression.

Day 1 –

Day 2 –

Day 3 –

Day 4 –

Day 5 –

Day 6 –

Day 7 –

Day 8 –

Day 9 –

....

Day 10 –

....

Day 11 –

....

Day 12 –

....

Day 13 –

....

Day 14 –

....

Day 15 –

....

Day 16 –

....

Day 17 –

....

Day 18 –

....

Day 19 –

....

Day 20 –

....

Day 21 –

Day 22 –

Day 23 –

Day 24 –

Day 25 –

Day 26 –

Day 27 –

Day 28 –

Day 29 –

Day 30 –

LOSS

GRIEF IS NOT A DISORDER, A
DISEASE OR A SIGN OF WEAKNESS.
IT IS AN EMOTIONAL, PHYSICAL AND
SPIRITUAL NECESSITY; THE PRICE
YOU PAY FOR LOVE. THE ONLY CURE
FOR GRIEF IS TO GRIEVE.

Earl Grollman

LOSS

Human logic understands the grief that follows a death. After a tragic accident with life-altering results, people can be sympathetic. With family relationships, unless they've been there, others probably won't get it. But involved or not, they'll most likely pick a side. People will often assume that you are the problem.

The truth is, broken or distant family relationships can feel like death, like loss. Sometimes, it feels like it would be easier emotionally if the family member(s) had died. Grieving the loss of a relationship is real. It's hard, and the internal anguish wrenches your soul.

Perhaps it's the future you're grieving—the things you were going to do. Maybe it's the past—all the childhood memories. Grief comes in waves. Go through every stage. Allow yourself time to grieve, and don't rush the process.

When the waves of loss swell over you, remember that it's okay to cry—women and men have emotions and tear ducts. You are grieving because you loved something precious and lost it. Those grief waves are also called "stages," and they have names: denial, anger, bargaining, depression, and acceptance.

Do Today:

If you've been holding back tears, allow yourself to cry.
If you've been upset with yourself for feeling the loss of a relationship,
give yourself permission to grieve.

LOSS

Day 1

ASK YOURSELF:

What have I lost that others may not be able to see? Am I more upset
about losing what was or what might be?

LOSS

SHAME

SHAME NEEDS THREE THINGS
TO GROW EXPONENTIALLY IN OUR
LIVES: SECRECY, SILENCE
AND JUDGMENT.

Brené Brown

SHAME

Have you ever bumped into someone (literally or online) who brought up a family member you've privately distanced from? Were you instantly flooded with shame? Were you embarrassed? It can be awkward. Sure, you and your family member aren't speaking to each other. That fact is painful enough, and now someone else is talking about them. They may know your business but not "your side" of the story. They may know nothing, and you find yourself tiptoeing around the topic.

Relationships generally fracture behind closed doors. The outside world knows only what they've been told from the perspective of the person telling it.

Here's the thing: You know why the relationship fell apart for you. You know your truth. If you've done your best to repair what remains of the relationship, if you were protecting an innocent, if you were taking the moral high ground, if you were refusing to be abused any longer, then you have nothing to be ashamed of! You have done nothing wrong.

Let that feeling of shame roll right off your shoulders. Silence its voice, its lies. Shame can control you only if you let it. Shame will keep you from living the life you were designed to live.

The next time you cross paths with that someone trying to shame you, or the next time you have that all-encompassing feeling, square your shoulders and stand with confidence. Allow the feeling to bring greater awareness. You will not live in shame; you don't need that extra weight. What is your truth—that thing you know confidently in your gut? What is your why?

Do Today:

Look in the mirror and speak your truth and why, out loud.
Say it again, louder this time.

SHAME

ASK YOURSELF:

Should I carry the shame of someone else's decision? Is this a burden I will let shape my identity? Why do I care what other people think or seek their approval?

SHAME

DAY 2

LONELINESS

DOES NOT COME FROM HAVING
NO PEOPLE AROUND YOU, BUT FROM
BEING UNABLE TO COMMUNICATE
THE THINGS THAT SEEM
IMPORTANT TO YOU.

Carl Jung

LONELINESS

A strained family relationship is a lonely place. If you've been rejected, betrayed, or ignored by loved ones, who can you talk to? You used to be able to pick up the phone and call your mom or text your sister. Now, that's gone. They don't want to hear from you. Or conversely, you have to maintain distance yourself because communication isn't healthy and may cause you to fall back into old habits.

Suffering knows no social boundaries. Loneliness eats away at the hearts of the most popular and the most ignored. We all want to be known and loved, and when the people who know us best and supposedly loved us the most are suddenly removed from our lives, by choice or happenstance, we can fall deeply into the pit of loneliness.

Gently walk through the feelings of loneliness showing kindness to yourself.

Do Today:

Call an old friend and talk about anything; better yet, meet someone for coffee and chat face-to-face. Join an online support community.

LONELINESS

Day 3

Ask Yourself:

What steps can I begin today to help myself with loneliness? When do
I feel the most alive and fulfilled?

LONELINESS

Day 3

FORGIVENESS

IS ME GIVING UP MY RIGHT TO
HURT YOU FOR HURTING ME.
FORGIVENESS IS THE FINAL
ACT OF LOVE.

Beyoncé

FORGIVENESS

Forgiveness—that's not a popular word. It can bring up old feelings and memories. But forgiveness doesn't give the offender a free pass. By forgiving, you aren't saying that the horrible thing never happened, that those words didn't cut you open, or that the abuse can be excused.

Forgiveness also doesn't mean allowing the offending person back in your life, whether in a different capacity or at all, permitting them to hurt you again, or removing a boundary. But when you don't forgive, that person still has power over you, and they are continuing to control your mind and choices. Their words or actions are still influencing you, echoing in your mind. The negativity is always there.

You forgive so that you, yourself, can complete the healing process. When you choose to forgive, you experience an internal release. Forgiveness is a step toward regaining control of your mental and emotional health.

Choosing not to forgive is like leaving a gaping wound open with no medical care. But through forgiveness, your wound can begin healing. Granted, there may always be a scar. Forgiveness doesn't erase your memories, but it does allow your soul to mend. It stops the bleeding and eases the pain.

You might not be ready to forgive just yet, and that's okay. Time is part of the process too.

Remember, forgiveness doesn't always manifest in words spoken to the offending person or to yourself. It may simply be a moment when you find healing through understanding and find yourself letting go of the pain because you no longer have to hold on to it.

Do Today:

Write down your hurt on a piece of paper. Say out loud, "I forgive you." Then throw that piece of paper away, flush it down the toilet, or toss it in a lake. In your mind, put up a "No fishing allowed" sign; you can't go back and get it.

FORGIVENESS

Day 4

ASK YOURSELF:

Will I be a better person, for myself, if I choose forgiveness?
Do I like the feelings unforgiveness brings me?
Is unforgiveness changing who I am?

FORGIVENESS

LOVE

HAS NOTHING TO DO WITH WHAT
YOU ARE EXPECTING TO GET—ONLY
WITH WHAT YOU ARE EXPECTING TO
GIVE—WHICH IS EVERYTHING.

Katharine Hepburn

LOVE

If someone would hurt you so deeply, did they truly love you in the first place? How can you be vulnerable and allow yourself to love others now? From now on, how do you know what love is and whether it's real?

Sometimes, we hurt those we love because we care so much and are trying too hard, and sometimes, we hurt people because we ourselves are hurting. Hurting people often hurt people. Each of us has our own life story. No one else has lived the exact sequence of events. Look at the person who hurt you. How have they been hurt? Did they adapt to life's struggles by becoming narcissistic or controlling? Are they just copy and pasting patterns of learned behavior?

Seeing their behaviors for what they really are will help you get the answers you need about love. Maybe that family member is genuinely incapable of pure love. Maybe they have no clue what love should look like, or maybe they made a mistake. And, yes, maybe they need to resolve their own internal conflict.

The bottom line is this: Whether there was or wasn't true love, that's not on you. You are not unlovable. You are worthy of being loved. You exist; therefore, you are valuable.

Do Today:

Define the word *love*.
What does love mean to you in word and in action?
How do you show what love should look like to those around you?

LOVE

DAY 5

Ask Yourself:

In what areas of my journey have I been demanding perfection of
myself or others? Must someone do or be something to deserve love?
Is love deserved by all people?
What family behavior patterns need to be addressed?

LOVE

GUILT

ISN'T ALWAYS A RATIONAL
THING . . . GUILT IS A WEIGHT THAT
WILL CRUSH YOU WHETHER YOU
DESERVE IT OR NOT.

Maureen Johnson

GUILT

Perhaps there is the nagging voice in the back of your mind, saying, *"If I'd only seen the signs sooner. Maybe I should have given one more chance. What if I was wrong? Did I actually set this in motion?"* Don't listen to that voice. It's guilt.

At the time you stepped away, did you believe you were doing what was right? Were you defending a child or setting boundaries for yourself? Ask yourself those questions and with honesty, evaluate your answers.

If you stood for what you believed in because you knew what was best for yourself or your family, tell guilt to disappear. Second-guessing yourself will only bring more pain.

If you were wronged—shunned, abused, mistreated, lied to, or left behind—that decision is not on you. The acting party is responsible for their actions. Don't own something that is not yours.

Guilt will keep you from progressing toward healing and wholeness. Guilt nags and gnaws at your mind. It holds you back, preventing you from moving forward.

Do Today:

Intentionally plan a trip to a store to buy yourself a little something. Treat yourself to your favorite dessert, binge on a couple episodes of a favorite show, or take some other simple action. Did you find yourself feeling guilty as you checked out at the register, took that first bite, or started the second (or third) episode? Why is that? Can you find joy in simply delighting in a little pleasure?

GUILT

Day 6

Ask Yourself:

What steps can I take to begin healing from this negative emotion? Is my feeling of guilt serving or hurting me and my journey to wholeness?

GUILT

Day 6

ABANDONMENT

DOESN'T HAVE THE SHARP BUT
DISSIPATING STING OF A SLAP.
IT'S LIKE A PUNCH TO THE GUT,
BRUISING YOUR SKIN AND DRIVING
THE PRECIOUS AIR FROM YOUR BODY.

Tayari Jones

ABANDONMENT

When your family turns against you, doesn't believe you, or won't support your choices, you may feel abandoned. If your parents walked away from you, if you chose a different lifestyle from your parents, or if you were rejected by your biological family, you may feel abandoned.

Often, people leave or ignore us because of their own personal conflicts. They simply cannot see past their own hurts or needs. But the flip side is that without knowing it, we can push people away, leading people to step back.

The yearning to know why you were abandoned can be maddening. Why would that person shut you out? Was there no true love? Was there no commitment? You may want to have an open conversation with the one who abandoned you, but such a conversation may not be possible or healthy. Always maintain proper boundaries.

If talking to the person isn't feasible or safe, consider talking to a trusted friend or mental health professional. It may be hard to talk to others about your feelings of abandonment. You know you're capable of making it without the other person—of making it on your own—but you don't want to have to.

Abandonment speaks volumes about the character of the person who stepped away from you. It takes wisdom and maturity to accept and love someone with whom we no longer agree. Their acceptance is not your problem; it's theirs.

Do Today:

Write a list of the people in your life who have left you and why you
believe they left. Now, write a list of people in your life who have
stayed and why you believe they have stayed.
Do you see any common themes?

ABANDONMENT

ASK YOURSELF:

What are the biggest changes in my life since feeling abandoned?
Which have been the most difficult? Has there been any good?

ABANDONMENT

DAY 7

ANGER

IS AN ACID THAT CAN DO MORE
HARM TO THE VESSEL IN WHICH IT
IS STORED THAN TO ANYTHING ON
WHICH IT IS POURED.

Mark Twain

ANGER

"How could they do this to me?"

"Why won't they believe me?"

No matter what the hurt, there will be anger. Abuse, cruel words, rejection, and secrets can make you angry, and there is nothing wrong with feeling anger. It is a valid emotion and one of the stages of grief. It's how you handle the anger that shows what you're made of.

Choose to rise above. Say no to shortsighted reactions and revenge. Don't let anger alter you as a person. It can destroy you and those you love.

Showing your anger through a harsh email, text, or conversation by voicing your initial thoughts and feelings without any time to regain your composure may not be a wise decision. Reacting thoughtlessly could invite even more pain into your life. Manage your anger rather than letting it control you. When you've been hurt by someone you love, anger is likely buried somewhere deep inside you. If you don't deal with it, it may surface when you least expect it and possibly hurt someone (or something) you're not upset with.

Uncharacteristic anger may surface as you walk through past trauma. Anger is nothing to fear. With care, allow yourself to process the new emotion as you learn to properly direct the feelings.

Do Today:

Compose a letter or email to the person who has hurt you. Now, wait a week or two, then review it. Could what you say be taken as volatile or reactive? Did you try to see the situation through their eyes too? Revise your wording. Wait another week and do the process again. Are your feelings the same? Now, it's up to you. Do you send it? Did this process help you find some healing?

ANGER

ASK YOURSELF:

Is my anger serving me well? Is this anger hurting or helping me? Am I more angry at myself or my loved one(s)?

ANGER

DAY 8

DISTRUST

IS LIKE A VICIOUS FIRE THAT
KEEPS GOING AND GOING, EVEN PUT
OUT, IT WILL REIGNITE ITSELF,
DEVOURING THE GOOD WITH
THE BAD, AND STILL FEEDING
ON EMPTY.

Anthony Liccione

DISTRUST

If your family can lie to you, can hurt you that deeply, can turn against you, then who can you trust? As in any relationship, it's not if but when you will be hurt because we all goof up sometimes. Distrust enters in when that hurt becomes abuse, manipulation, or lies. Once trust has been broken, it is extremely difficult to regain. But through time and with proper boundaries, it can be done.

Trusting your feelings will take time. Don't allow yourself to fall into the trap of distrusting everyone and everything. Distrust can quickly become a landslide eroding any relationship going forward. It can become the silent third party that creates undesirable triangulation in future relationships. Learning to trust might feel like learning to love again too. When you trust people, your whole world can fill up with new experiences. Don't shut people out.

Look at the people who are still in your life; look at their behavior patterns. Have they shown their trustworthiness? Do they love you? If so, they are worth the risk.

Do Today:

Has someone proven faithful to you through this journey?
Open up to them. Talk to them about how you feel and
how you want to trust them.

DISTRUST

ASK YOURSELF:

What makes someone trustworthy?
What boundaries do I need to put in place to start trusting an
individual or people again? Can I trust myself?

DISTRUST

DAY 9

PAIN

THAT'S THE THING ABOUT PAIN, IT DEMANDS TO BE FELT.

John Green

PAIN

It really, really hurts. Pain is unexplainable some days. As waves of reality collide, the pain is so intense you can't breathe.

You cycle through every emotion possible, crying until your tears run dry. With your jaw clenched, your chest heaves as you draw deep breaths. All you can say is, "Why?"

Let the pain teach you. It can show you so much about yourself. You'll learn what's important to you and why. You'll learn your own limitations and boundaries. Don't run from the pain; sit with it. Don't fight the pain. Use this season to gain self-awareness.

Instead of letting the pain control you, let it guide you to a stronger understanding of yourself. Feeling pain doesn't mean you're weak; it means you're strong. It means you've taken risks with your heart and are doing something worth fighting for right now.

Do Today:

Pick up a pencil and draw or write out what your pain looks like.
Get as detailed or abstract as you'd like. There is no right or wrong.

PAIN

ASK YOURSELF:

Why haven't I let myself feel this hurt?
What am I afraid will happen when I do?
How do I respond when I begin to feel emotional pain?

PAIN

TRIGGERS

ARE LIKE LITTLE PSYCHIC
EXPLOSIONS THAT CRASH THROUGH
AVOIDANCE AND BRING THE
DISSOCIATED, AVOIDED TRAUMA
SUDDENLY, UNEXPECTEDLY, BACK
INTO CONSCIOUSNESS.

Carolyn Spring

TRIGGERS

Almost anything can trigger painful memories or thoughts: a person with similar characteristics, a familiar situation or smell or song or place or feeling—even social media. For some, the triggering moment may end in an all-out anxiety attack. Others might cry or feel their heart race. Whatever emotional or physical sensation you experience, it's a natural reaction to a trauma memory.

It's possible that you will feel triggered for a very long time. Sometimes, on a journey of healing and restoration, you have to dig pretty deep, stimulating buried memories you may have archived. Triggers can show up even years down the road when you least expect them.

Triggers are signs that we still have work to do in order to heal. What you are feeling is very real and completely normal.

Do Today:

Remember back to the last time you felt triggered and answer a few questions. (If this is too painful, it's okay.) What brought that moment on? What thoughts were scurrying through your mind? What did you feel physically? In what areas do you think you still need healing?

TRIGGERS

ASK YOURSELF:

Am I putting myself in situations that are not healthy for me emotionally? Am I allowing my emotions to set the pace, or am I self-regulating when I sense a trigger? Do I think I am worthy of being safe—physically, emotionally, and mentally?

TRIGGERS

DAY 11

REBUILDING

The secret of change is to
focus all of your energy not on
fighting the old,
but on building the new.

Socrates

REBUILDING

Is the relationship with your family member(s) salvageable? After making apologies and talking it out, look to the future. Don't allow yourself to go back to those old hurts. Set new boundaries and stick to them.

If the family relationship can't be repaired right now, you may need to rebuild your own soul. Take time for self-care. It's not a waste of time, and it's not selfish. In this season you can find healing from hurts while establishing new healthy goals and boundaries for yourself.

Remember, what happened changed the course of tomorrow, but it does not need to control you moving forward. There is a new life full of love ahead of you. Have patience with yourself in this time.

Do Today:

Write down a list of how you would like your relationship (with your family or an individual) to look if you both took steps toward rebuilding your relationship. Next, write down a list of how things used to look. What do you want future relationships to look like?

REBUILDING

ASK YOURSELF:

What new boundaries will be needed going forward?
How will I protect myself from being hurt in this way again?
What was I tolerating before?
How will I prioritize my needs in the future?

REBUILDING

DAY 12

LONGING

You really didn't see the sadness or the longing unless you already knew it was there. But that was the trick, wasn't it? Everyone had their disappointment and their baggage; only, some people carried it in their inside pockets and not on their backs.

Maggie Stiefvater

LONGING

Even if you know you were right to break away or if they walked away from you, you will miss your family. They were your tribe. All your childhood or many of life's memories circulate around them. They cheered when you got your driver's license. They lent you the money for a down payment on your first house. Your uncle always used to tell that same crazy story every time he saw you, and you miss that. Your grandma always tried to feed you more than you could handle, and you wish she was there to fill your plate. Your brother or sister constantly picked on you, but now you'd give anything for them to razz you just a little bit. Your spouse raised the kids with you "back when."

You can't control others or their decisions; you can only control yourself. But that longing for those you've lost may easily turn to tears. You miss your family; you're homesick. Your heart yearns to be at peace with them again, but it's over. You long to speak with them, your arms want to hug them again, and you ache to tell them how much you love them.

That longing is a sign of love, of hope for a better future, of gratitude for days gone by.

Do Today:

You know that thing you've been wanting to do for a long time now?
Today is the day to make it happen. This is something you can control.

LONGING

Ask Yourself:

What is it I really want? What void am I trying to fill?
How can I regain my peace of mind?
Will it be okay if this relationship is never completely healed?

LONGING

SELF-DOUBT

I HAVE SELF-DOUBT. I HAVE INSECURITY. I HAVE FEAR OF FAILURE. I HAVE NIGHTS WHEN I SHOW UP AT THE ARENA AND I'M LIKE, "MY BACK HURTS, MY FEET HURT, MY KNEES HURT. I DON'T HAVE IT. I JUST WANT TO CHILL." WE ALL HAVE SELF-DOUBT. YOU DON'T DENY IT, BUT YOU ALSO DON'T CAPITULATE TO IT. YOU EMBRACE IT.

Kobe Bryant

SELF-DOUBT

"Wait. Maybe I imagined it. Maybe they didn't really say or do that hurtful thing. Maybe it was my fault. Am I being too sensitive? They didn't mean it, did they?"

Sometimes, we want so much for something to be or not be true that we allow our memories to become skewed. Lists and lists of questions flood our minds.

Stand firm. When you decided to place boundaries in the relationship, when you approached your loved one asking for answers, when you refused to apologize for your life choices, did you do so with the intention of hurting someone or with a heart of pure love?

You see, there's a difference between making a decision that might cause someone pain for the greater good and making a decision that will intentionally cause pain so that you can get even or watch someone squirm or suffer.

Don't doubt yourself when things get crazy. If you made a mistake, you can handle it and strive to make amends. Self-doubt is an insecurity. You were confident when you took your position. Continue in that confidence.

Do Today:

Remember the last time you had a gut feeling about something and
you were right? Or that time you took a risk and it paid off? Think back
to your successes knowing that you are strong and capable.
Go forward with surety.

SELF-DOUBT

DAY 14

Ask Yourself:

What is it I am most afraid of happening? What if that does happen?
What's the best/worst-case scenario?

SELF-DOUBT

IDENTITY

LIFE ISN'T ABOUT
FINDING YOURSELF.

LIFE IS ABOUT CREATING YOURSELF.

George Bernard Shaw

IDENTITY

Family is part of our identity, but it is far more than the people who raised you. We often think that who we are is tied to a family name, city, race, religion, or even an educational institution because it's in our DNA to need community. When something challenges a connection to a person, idea, or belief that has always been part of us, it also challenges our identity or sense of self.

"If biologically I am not a _____, then who am I?"

"If my views on my faith are changing, what good is a confused, floundering person?"

"My brother won't speak to me because he doesn't agree with my choices. I'm such a failure."

You are so much more than how you were raised, where you live, the color of your skin, your level of education, or who agrees with you or not. Those things are influences for certain, but ultimately, you are the one who is making decisions about your present and your future.

You are valuable because you are a human being. You are free to decide who you will be.

Do Today:

Let's do some deep digging today into what makes you you.
Write down your answers to these questions:

What are your core values? What is a calling of your life? What makes
you come alive? What do you need to feel completely whole as an
individual? Where are you getting your sense of worth and why?
Whose voice is constantly in your head? Why them?

IDENTITY

ASK YOURSELF:

Why is my identity important? Did I stop being me when this happened? Should I let this situation define who I will be in the future? What parts of who I was, or thought I was, weren't actually what I wanted?

IDENTITY

DAY 15

TRUST

NATURE HAS PLANTED IN OUR
MINDS AN INSATIABLE LONGING TO
SEE THE TRUTH.

Marcus Tullius Cicero

TRUST

Trust is the foundation of successful human relationships. The reality is that no matter how much we love people, we eventually hurt or are hurt by someone.

We trust the other drivers on the freeway not to hit us. We trust the workers at the restaurant to give us safe food to eat. We trust our doctor to have the skills required for surgery. We trust our religious leaders to speak truth to us.

If you can't trust your family anymore, who can you trust? If your spouse of so many years can turn their back on you, you may feel as though you can never trust anyone again.

Trust is earned. People can earn back that trust, but not necessarily the same people who've lost it. If there is a pattern of unhealthy or toxic behavior, establish boundaries to protect yourself. If there was a one-time offense and the other person is willing to work toward reconciliation, consider taking the opportunity also with the proper boundaries. Sometimes, though, the offense was too egregious, and you cannot and should not fully restore trust.

When there is a seed of doubt about someone's motives, faithfulness, or honesty, the relationship can struggle, even if only inside your own heart and mind. You may risk additional pain and possible abuse. If you've been wounded by someone, it's okay to step away for a season to decide whether the person is able to earn your trust once more. Know that you will be able to trust other people again in time.

Do Today:

Write down the three most important aspects of trust to you, your nonnegotiables. How were these broken?

TRUST

ASK YOURSELF:

Could it ever be possible to trust my family or the
individual again? What evidence do I need to see that will
show me they are worthy of my trust? Is the broken trust
in this relationship affecting how I trust others?

TRUST

FLASHBACKS

THINK OF THE FLASHBACK AS A
CLUE TO THE NEXT PIECE OF WORK.
NO MATTER HOW PAINFUL, TRY TO
VIEW IT AS A POSITIVE INDICATION
THAT YOU ARE NOW READY AND
WILLING TO REMEMBER.

Beverly Engel

FLASHBACKS

In the middle of the night, you jolt awake. All your past pain played out again in your dreams. Now, your heart is pounding, your breath quickening, and your body sweating.

Flashbacks can often be nearly as difficult as the experience itself. We can repress painful memories, but the physical and emotional sensors are still alive and active in our subconscious. While flashbacks can feel very real, they are only a memory. You are not actually being hurt all over again, just remembering the hurt.

Flashbacks can be evidence that a wound hasn't healed yet. Over time, they may lessen as you take steps toward wholeness. Other times, your trauma may be so intense that you will need help learning how to manage the flashbacks.

Do Today:

What is that one thing you have stopped yourself from feeling?
Today is the day to allow yourself to go there. Find a place where you
feel safe and let the emotion happen.

FLASHBACKS

DAY 17

ASK YOURSELF:

What thoughts race through my mind in that
flashback moment? What am I feeling? What actions do I need
to take to begin healing? Do I need to speak with a professional
about the intensity of my flashbacks?

FLASHBACKS

DAY 17

DISBELIEF

TRUTH WILL ALWAYS BE TRUTH,
REGARDLESS OF LACK OF
UNDERSTANDING,
DISBELIEF OR IGNORANCE.

W. Clement Stone

DISBELIEF

Wait, what just happened? Do you ever question your own memory? When you replay the scenario in your mind, does the screen go blank or fuzzy, filling you with uncertainty? Are you in a state of shock, not trusting yourself?

When a family relationship is broken, it's often hard to believe. Your family brought you into this world and witnessed all your firsts. They supported you through college and went all gaga with the birth of your child. How could they just suddenly not be there? You anticipated that conflict was part of the average family. But this—you could not have seen this coming.

It all feels unbelievable, and the temptation is to beat yourself up for "missing all the signs." Disbelief is part of the grief process, but don't be gaslighted by your own emotions or alternate versions of your story. What happened, happened. Don't let your emotions inhibit your intuition. Listen to your gut.

Do Today:

What is that one thing you have stopped yourself from feeling?
Today is the day to allow yourself to go there. Find a place where you
feel safe and let the emotion happen.

DISBELIEF

ASK YOURSELF:

Am I more surprised at the event itself or the person/people involved?
Am I questioning my part in this or whether it really happened?

DISBELIEF

DAY 18

EMPTINESS

WHICH IS CONCEPTUALLY
LIABLE TO BE MISTAKEN FOR
SHEER NOTHINGNESS IS IN FACT
THE RESERVOIR OF INFINITE
POSSIBILITIES.

Daisetz Teitaro Suzuki

EMPTINESS

DAY 19

Did you wake up today feeling nothing? Is your energy gone and your hope for the future squelched? Perhaps last night was a sleepless night of tears and you are spent, with nothing left to give to others or yourself.

That feeling of emptiness is the emotional reality that something was truly taken from you. There is a hole in your life now. Who you knew, what you knew—that's all changed. Perhaps you need to grieve the loss of what you thought was reality or the fact that you now feel alone in this journey.

When your emotions are exhausted and your body is tired, the sense of emptiness can become more prominent. Allow yourself to take the time to rest your body, mind, and emotions.

Do Today:

Do something today that fills your heart with joy or
helps someone else. Set up your art easel and paint, pull out
that guitar and play your favorite tunes, volunteer at a pet shelter,
or help the elderly neighbor across the street mow their grass.
Taking a nap can also be a good way to fill back up.

EMPTINESS

ASK YOURSELF:

What actions make me feel full or satisfied in my life?
Specifically, what was removed from my life that was filling me?
Does that person, idea, or lifestyle determine my value?
What can I do to replace the emptiness with joy?

EMPTINESS

DAY 19

NUMBNESS

BY DEFAULT, MOST OF US HAVE
TAKEN THE DARE TO SIMPLY
SURVIVE. EXIST. GET THROUGH.
FOR THE MOST PART, WE LIVE
NUMB TO LIFE—WE'VE GROWN
WEARY AND APATHETIC AND
JADED . . . AND WOUNDED.

Ann Voskamp

NUMBNESS

After a trauma, shock, or unexpected turn of events, there often comes a season of numbness. You may not know what you feel or even how to feel. Honestly, you may not even care.

With so many pieces to the puzzle of our lives, we can't expect everything to always fit together in a perfect picture or to process overnight. After a time of reflection, we can better fit the new pieces while we learn to understand our emotions and what sparked them.

When feelings do return—anger, bitterness, hurt, fear, shame—know that there is no wrong emotion. You are allowed to feel them all. But do remember this: Knee-jerk emotional reactions can lead to mistakes; responding after thoughtful consideration produces better results.

Your emotions are not severed. Your feelings are not cauterized. They are just tired. Rest. The emotions will return.

Do Today:

Find a quiet spot at home, in a park, or in your favorite coffee shop.
Set a timer for 15 minutes. Do not try to feel anything. Sit quietly.
If a feeling comes, curiously follow it through. If not,
allow your soul to accept the stillness.

NUMBNESS

DAY 20

ASK YOURSELF:

What thoughts am I avoiding? By denying my emotions, am I trying to protect myself from further hurt? What positive measures will I take when I do feel emotions again?

NUMBNESS

DAY 20

BREATHE

SOMETIMES THE MOST IMPORTANT
THING IN A WHOLE DAY IS THE
REST WE TAKE BETWEEN TWO DEEP
BREATHS.

Etty Hillesum

BREATHE

You're crying so hard you can't breathe. You feel as though an elephant is sitting on your chest. You find yourself holding your breath or feeling like someone just punched you in the gut.

It's an instinct to hold your breath when you're upset, angry, or hurt. Holding your breath is also a physical sign of shock or surprise and doing so may activate your fight-or-flight reaction.

Children will sometime hold their breath to earn a caregiver's attention—possibly a sign of underlying needs. We hold our breath when we swim so that we don't drown or when we smell a foul odor so that we don't get sick. We hold our breath after an injury or accident—those we witness or experience. We hold our breath when the ball leaves the three-point line headed directly into the basket right as the buzzer sounds. Breath is intrinsically tied to our experiences of fear or anticipation.

Like our breath, we can hold our trauma inside our bodies. We need to allow the trauma to be released, just like an exhale. Movement through dance, creative arts, and activities such as yoga can help you to move that trapped trauma along.

Do Today:

Select a quiet place where you feel safe. Listen to the silence and allow it to relax you. Slowly take a deep breath in and hold it in for a few seconds. Calmly let it out while tuning into what you feel physically. Take another slow deep breath and hold it a little longer this time. Let it out slowly. What did you feel emotionally? Repeat this practice a few more times, really focusing on what you feel.

BREATHE

Day 21

ASK YOURSELF:

Am I allowing my situation to keep me from feeling peace? Are my emotions wound so tightly that they are restricting even my natural breathing? What trauma have I kept stored inside my body?

BREATHE

DAY 21

HOPE

IS THE THING WITH FEATHERS
THAT PERCHES IN THE SOUL AND
SINGS THE TUNE WITHOUT THE
WORDS AND NEVER STOPS AT ALL.

Emily Dickinson

HOPE

Hopeless has been called the saddest word in the English language. Your family member made poor decisions, behaved hurtfully, or directly betrayed you. It feels as though the relationship will never mend, that there's no hope.

When you lose hope, life often feels meaningless. A gray cloud encompasses your every feeling and thought. What happens when nothing changes for days, months, or years? What if the others involved are never willing to reconcile? What if the necessary boundaries do not involve mending the relationship?

The pain for everyone may take a long time to heal. In the meantime, hope. Hope is what futures are built upon. Hope that things will get better, that someday a relationship could mend, that someone will invent a cure, that you will embrace your loved one again, that you will find healing.

Do Today:

What are you hopeful for today? Write down five things. Now, write down three emotions you feel when you look forward to those things. Watch a feel-good movie or a show that makes you laugh.

HOPE

Ask Yourself:

Who are the most hopeful people I know?
How can I be influenced by them?

HOPE

PEACE

DO NOT LET THE BEHAVIOR
OF OTHERS DESTROY YOUR
INNER PEACE.

Dalai Lama

PEACE

You just want to feel like you again. You want to sleep at night. Instead, your mind races; you spend the dark hours researching, praying, or pacing the floor.

Bruised relationships, trauma, or loss can steal your peace. The agonizing memories can do more than break your heart: They can break your mind and soul, if you let them. When peace eludes you, anxiety, depression, anger, and lethargy fill the void and threaten even your physical health.

There are days when you try to shake the gnawing, dark feelings off, but they won't go away. In fact, the more you fight them, the more stubborn and strong they become.

But here's the truth: No one can steal your peace unless you allow it. You are in charge of your peace.

Do Today:

Turn on an upbeat song—a song that always makes you
want to dance. Now, move your body. If you're a dancer, groove
away! If you're not, just move your arms and legs or clap your hands
together. Release control of your mind and body just for
the length of this song. Let the music set the mood.

PEACE

Can I control my situation? Or more importantly, do I need to? If I cannot control this, what will happen in my life? What am I in control of this very minute? I feel most peaceful when_____.

PEACE

DAY 23

VULNERABILITY

SECURITY IS MOSTLY A
SUPERSTITION.
IT DOES NOT EXIST IN NATURE, NOR
DO THE CHILDREN OF MEN AS A
WHOLE EXPERIENCE IT. AVOIDING
DANGER IS NO SAFER IN THE LONG
RUN THAN OUTRIGHT EXPOSURE.
THE FEARFUL ARE CAUGHT AS
OFTEN AS THE BOLD.

Helen Keller

VULNERABILITY

There are phrases we use to avoid the word vulnerable: "Let your hair down" or "Let yourself go." Inside these kinds of expressions is a hidden theme—releasing control. After you have been hurt, opening yourself up again is hard. You are not in control of what happens next. Allowing yourself to be vulnerable again may be a battle.

What *might* happen if you let your guard down plagues your mind. Will people accept or reject you? Will the hurt be repeated?

Revealing your true self after having your heart injured takes courage. Sharing your story or even seeking counsel can feel overwhelming. When you hear yourself saying things out loud for the first time about how you *really* feel or what you have experienced, it can be a moment of clarity and liberation.

Do Today:

Pay it forward this week at the coffee shop, drive-through, or grocery store. Was that a moment of vulnerability, or did it come easily?

VULNERABILITY

Ask Yourself:

Am I afraid of doing or saying something out of fear
of being judged by others? Am I being honest with myself about
what I am feeling or what I want? Where is a safe place that
I can practice being vulnerable—in a support group,
with a close friend, with my significant other?

VULNERABILITY

Day 24

CHOICES

LITTLE PROGRESS CAN BE MADE BY
MERELY ATTEMPTING TO REPRESS
WHAT IS EVIL. OUR GREAT HOPE
LIES IN DEVELOPING WHAT IS GOOD.

Calvin Coolidge

CHOICES

Choices are personal. We make them every day. And remember: Not making a choice is still a choice.

"The blue shirt or the gray?"

"Should I wear loafers or tennis shoes?"

"Smoothie or latte?"

"Scream at the driver in front of me or calmly listen to my audio book?"

"Flirt with that girl at the office or walk the other way?"

"Go to counseling or battle through it alone?"

Every decision we make might seem independent of another, but every choice is truly connected. One bad choice leads to another, and vice versa. We can fall into choice habits—especially toward whatever is easiest; gets the adrenaline rushing; is most fun, predictable, or comfortable.

You cannot control other people or their decisions, but you can own your past choices. And purpose to make better ones today.

Do Today:

What decision have you been putting off?
Write it down on a piece of paper and stick it to your bathroom mirror.
Today might be the day for you to choose.

CHOICES

DAY 25

ASK YOURSELF:

Is there a pattern of decision-making in my life?
How do I make my choices? Do I follow through or give up?

CHOICES

DAY 25

NORMALCY

IT WAS INEVITABLE FOR PEOPLE
TO TRY TO CREATE A SENSE OF
NORMALCY IN A PLACE WHERE
NOTHING WAS NORMAL. IT HELPED
ONE GET THROUGH THE DAY, TO ADD
PREDICTABILITY TO A LIFE THAT
WAS INHERENTLY UNPREDICTABLE.

Nicholas Sparks

NORMALCY

When will the pain end? The triggers and the questions? Is there ever going to be a time when the hurt isn't foremost in your mind?

The answer is yes.

As the old adage says, "Time heals all wounds." However, you can't hurry the healing, and scars will remain. There's no going back, but there is a going forward with a new normal. The life you once knew is gone. Why would you want to go back? You're growing every day! Normalcy is subjective. Don't get stuck wanting what used to be.

Embrace this new discovery. Perhaps a loved one showed their true colors, or your family revealed a long-hidden truth. Look forward to the new normal—one of truth. Don't fear it. Claim it.

Do Today:

Draw a big circle. Now stare at it for a few seconds.
This is your future, and you get to decide how it will look. What do
you want it to include? Whom do you want it to include? Write down
your thoughts inside the circle. It's your storyboard.

NORMALCY

ASK YOURSELF:

What about "the way things used to be" do I miss now?
What are some things I can look forward to in the new normal?

NORMALCY

DAY 26

HYPOCRISY

GOD HATH GIVEN YOU
ONE FACE, AND YOU MAKE
YOURSELF ANOTHER.

William Shakespeare

HYPOCRISY

All your life, you knew one reality, one truth. Then a revelation, situation, event, or tragedy occurred, and suddenly your family is changed forever. The truth is out. Your childhood was all a well-crafted story designed to protect someone else, a reputation, or way of thinking.

Families often have a set of standards or expectations in place, spoken or understood. Those guidelines might be based in religious beliefs or family and cultural tradition. When those expected values are violated, you can find yourself in a state of shock. Anger or betrayal might mix with grief or denial. All you feel is the hypocrisy:

They were one way at home but apparently a different person at school. They had been sneaking around behind your back and covering their tracks for months, all while acting like a good spouse. They abused a child. They all knew the truth, but no one ever told you. They taught you honesty, fidelity, and ethics, but they sold you a false narrative because they broke their vows and embezzled family money. They _____ (fill in the blank).

Do Today:

Put yourself in the other person's shoes for a minute.
Separate the person from their action. Imagine that you are
faced with the same choices. Were the expectations of the family or
culture different than they are now? What consequences would they
have accepted had they made a different choice? Is what they did
immoral or just what they believed was best at the time?
What hurts have they suffered in their own past?

HYPOCRISY

Day 27

ASK YOURSELF:

Am I being a hypocrite to myself by not being honest
about my feelings? Am I being a hypocrite if I don't tell anyone
about what happened? Is this what's best for other parties involved?
What actions do I need to make for my own healing? Is there any
legal action I am avoiding because I am afraid?

HYPOCRISY

DAY 27

LIES

IF YOU TELL THE TRUTH,
YOU DON'T HAVE TO REMEMBER
ANYTHING.

Mark Twain

LIES

"Until death do us part?"
"You always knew he wasn't my dad?"
"Why did you lie to me about our finances?"
"Wait, it was all a made-up story?"
"But you taught me this was truth."

Whatever untruth you have discovered, it hurts. You were deceived. Someone went back on their word, withheld truth from you, or propagated the lies they have believed themselves.

People can be pathological liars, sneaky and dishonest about even the smallest of things. Some people lie to protect others, without realizing the long-term pain those lies will cause. Others lie without understanding that their beliefs are a deception.

The deceit might be a one-time deal, but lies and uncovered truths can shake you to the core and shatter your trust in everyone and everything. A breach of trust suspends you in uncertainty about your past, your relationships, your choices. You question everything. What else is a lie? How much of your life is based on partial truths? Your foundation is cracked, and you feel as though the whole floor could give way at any second.

Stand firm on what is true in your story: You didn't choose this. You didn't make this decision. You didn't participate knowingly. You are not a liar. You are going to survive this.

Do Today:

Write out the numbers 1 to 10 on a line.
Circle the number that shows how much you trusted the person before
you discovered the lie. What number would you choose now?

LIES

ASK YOURSELF:

Was this lie designed to hurt me? What hurts the most about this deception? When was the first time I was deceived or duped (that I can remember)? How did I handle my feelings? What made me open to trusting people again? Is there anyone I still trust?

LIES

QUESTIONS

Remember, an easy question can have an easy answer. But a hard question must have a hard answer. And for the hardest questions of all, there may be no answer—except faith.

Charles Sheffield

QUESTIONS

"Why did this happen? Why did they do this? Why am I feeling this way?"

You've started gritting your teeth. The hurt is so deep, and you just want to know why it happened. It's nearly unbearable. When you suffer pain or deception, you have questions. Everything feels muddled.

You may believe that your questions should have answers—that you deserve answers, whether medically, financially, spiritually, psychologically, or any other matter. Demanding an answer may not always achieve the results you desire. Sometimes, answers are elusive. They may take time or prove impossible to locate.

Questions are a natural part of the healing process. Your heart believes that answers will help you make sense of a traumatic situation. In reality, there may not be an answer. The person who hurt you may not know the truth or may not share it because of their own pain, selfishness, hate, or fear of vulnerability. Choose not to allow unanswered questions to hinder your personal healing and growth.

Do Today:

What questions do you long to have answered about yourself, your situation, or the other people in your story? Write them down. Categorize them if you can. Circle the questions that involve only you.

QUESTIONS

Ask Yourself:

If I never get the answers I want, can I move forward?
Why is it so important to me to have my questions answered?

QUESTIONS

REVIVE

And so with the sunshine and the great bursts of leaves growing on the trees, just as things grow in fast movies, I had that familiar conviction that life was beginning over again with the summer.

F. Scott Fitzgerald

REVIVE

Today just felt different. There was a bounce in your step, and hope was flitting around your heart like a butterfly. After a breakthrough, it feels like that first crisp autumn morning or an ice-cold lemonade on a summer day. Did you find yourself putting on makeup or shaving for the first time in a while? Did you exchange your lounge pants for a snazzy pair of jeans?

The sense of being revived isn't planned, but it is the result of hard work. You may finally feel peace or joy. For the first time in a long time, getting through the day wasn't hard. You've faced demons and come out on the other side.

Having the feeling of revival does not mean that all the hard times are over and that you'll never experience the old pain again. Rather, feeling revived, even for just a day or a moment, shows that you're healing, renewing your sense of hope, achieving clarity, and are creating a new normal. Life is full of good and bad days, good and bad situations. You've survived them, and you will survive more. You're stronger now.

Do Today:

Take a deep breath. Now, commit to something
you've been considering—an online course, an in-person class,
a volunteer position, or an audition. Choose an activity to do
once a week for the next month (e.g., "Every Friday
night, I will eat my favorite ice cream.").

REVIVE

ASK YOURSELF:

How has my perspective about myself and my family changed
in the last 30 days? What can I look forward to in the next few weeks?
What is important for me to do next?

REVIVE

Day 30

ABOUT THE AUTHOR

For over two decades, Rebekah's skills, passions, and leadership have taken her around the globe to work with nonprofits and other organizations. Her background includes educational and online content development, event coordinating, international relations, and public speaking.

Currently, Rebekah is the director of public relations for NPE Friends Fellowship, an international nonprofit organization that supports individuals and their families who have received unexpected results from an at-home DNA test.

She is also a consultant, writer, and advocate supporting survivors of spiritual abuse by providing resources to educate and equip not only the survivors, but the public as well. Sharing her story to help others who have had similar life experiences is at the heart of Rebekah's purpose.

Rebekah holds a BA in urban ministry and family crisis with a counseling minor and an MA in religious education; she is a Certified Professional Life Coach. She has worked with news sources including BBC, NBC, and ABC, and a variety of other platforms such as podcasts and film projects.

Her hobbies include binge-watching riveting shows, thrifting with her family, traveling internationally, and dabbling in all things creative and artistic. Rebekah and her family reside in Texas.

You can connect with Rebekah via her website: RebekahDrumsta.com.

 @DrumstaRebekah @RebekahDrumsta @DrumstaRebekah

Printed in the USA
CPSIA information can be obtained
at www.ICGtesting.com
LVHW060007260824
789243LV00011B/636